TESTIMONIALS

"Dr. Meadows is one of the most passionate investors I know. Not only is he constantly expanding his knowledge about various investment strategies and vehicles, but he is equally as passionate about sharing his knowledge with others. Knowledge is power, and Dr. Meadows is committed to sharing invaluable information that helps individuals empower themselves as well as their families."

—Johnnie Dee Swain III
President and Founder of Swain Foods LLC and
Swain Farms Co.

"Dr. Kenyon Meadows helps investors and entrepreneurs see their environment in a new way and imagine the potential and possibilities for navigating it."

—Robert L. Brantley, MBA
Managing Member, The Brantley Group

"Dr. Meadows's desire to educate me as a new investor has opened my eyes to investment opportunities that I would have never known about with my mutual fund advisor."

—Thomas Mager, MD
Director, Division of Quality of Emergency Medicine
Summa Akron City Hospital

"Dr. Meadows's passion to encourage and educate novice investors is refreshing. His candid approach and willingness to share invaluable information has helped my family tremendously."

—Ernest Burt, PhD
Director of Online Programs
Everglades University

ALTERNATIVE
FINANCIAL MEDICINE

HIGH-YIELD INVESTING IN A LOW-YIELD WORLD

KENYON MEADOWS, M.D.

MEADOWS
ENTERPRISES

St. Simon Island, GA

Meadows Enterprises Press
252 St. James Ave.
St. Simons Island, GA 31522
k.meadows@yahoo.com

Editorial team: Author Bridge Media, www.AuthorBridgeMedia.com
Project Manager and Editorial Director: Helen Chang
Editor: Katherine MacKenett
Publishing Manager: Laurie Aranda

Library of Congress Control Number: 2016904063
ISBN: 978-0-9970040-0-7 – Softcover
978-0-9970040-1-4 – hardcover
978-0-9970040-2-1 – ebook

Ordering Information:
Quantity sales: Special discounts are available on quantity purchases by corporations, associations, and others. For details, contact the publisher at the address above.

In gratitude for the desire to achieve,
I dedicate this book to:
God, who put it in me;
Mom, who nurtured it;
My wife Wilnita, who supports it;
and Camille and Gabrielle, who will carry it on.

ACKNOWLEDGMENTS

First and foremost, I want to acknowledge my immediate family, Wilnita, Camille, and Gabrielle. Thank you for allowing me the time and giving me the support to complete this project.

I thank my digital mentors, whose online content was my springboard into the world of alternative investing and financial technology.

I am grateful to Peter Renton and Dara Albright, cofounders of the Lendit Conference. I watched every second of your video content multiple times. Without it, there would be no *Alternative Financial Medicine* project.

Ron Suber of Prosper.com has my gratitude. Your visionary keynotes have been a source of constant inspiration to me.

I am likewise grateful to Jilliene Hellman of Realty-Mogul. You make real estate crowdfunding seem like the coolest investment anyone could make.

To Mike Cagney and Dan Macklin, thanks for bringing a much-needed infusion of sophistication and common sense to the student loan market.

Finally, I'd like to thank a whole host of other entrepreneurs and investors with robust online presences who have taught me so much over the years. In no particular order: Gary Vaynerchuk, Glendon Cameron, Robert Kiyosaki, Dr. Dennis Bethel, Kathy Fettke, Pat Flynn, Brandon Turner, Josh Dorkin, Tai Lopez, Dr. David Phelps, Jason Hartman, Grant Cardone, Boyce Watkins, and many others.

Contents

Chapter 1

Introduction

My Two Financial Problems:
Volatility and Low Yield

If you have been reasonably thoughtful about your finances, you may have come to the same conclusion I did a few years ago: the traditional methods of savings and investment haven't been working well in recent years for the average person.

After an unprecedented twenty-year bull run from 1980 to 2000 in which it was difficult not to make money, the stock market has been less than stellar over the past fifteen years. Owing in large part to the tech bubble of 2001 and the mortgage/credit crisis of 2008, the net return of the broad S&P 500 Index since 2000 has been about 2 percent after adjusting for inflation and fees. That seemed like a pretty meager return considering all of the volatility you were subjecting your money to.

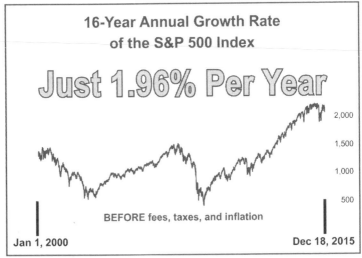

What about those of us who are more risk averse and prefer to try to save money as opposed to investing it in the market? When you look back on interest rates paid on savings accounts stretching back to the early 1970s, rates north of 8 percent were common, with a peak of 21.5 percent in 1980! Contrast that with our present economic state, where since 2008 we have had what is known as a zero interest rate policy. One of the main mandates of the Federal Reserve since the mortgage crisis of 2008 has been to get banks' balance sheets back in order. In order to do that, the Fed has radically lowered the rate it charges banks to borrow money, known as the federal funds rate, which has effectively been in the 0.25 to 0.5 percent range.

While that has been great for banks, it has not been very positive for savers, who have been forced to endure interest rates below 1 percent on their accounts. When you consider the fact that the official inflation rate is around 2 percent, and some sources calculate 3 to 4 percent as a more realistic measure, you can clearly see that the purchasing power of the money in your savings account is being eroded away.

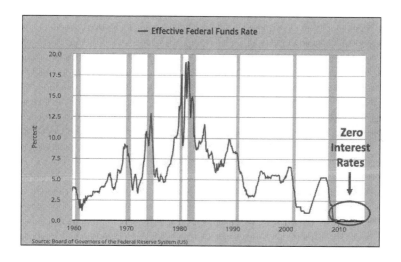

While it was interesting to learn about all of this economic history, I didn't put a plan of action in place to remedy its negative effects until I had an encounter with an old acquaintance whose life circumstances put a face on the problem.

A Wake-Up Call

Like many of you, I have a 401(k) through my job that is invested traditional paper assets, in my case, primarily mutual funds. In addition to this, I used to devote a significant amount of my disposable income to purchasing individual securities through a separate brokerage account. By 2008, I'd built up what I thought was a well-diversified portfolio ranging across growth stocks, blue chips, and low-risk bonds. But that year, like everyone else, I saw my portfolio take a nearly 40 percent hit.

Yeah. Ouch.

"You are young," everyone kept telling me. "You've got plenty of time for the market to bounce back." And indeed it has. But what if I had been much further down the road in life when the market decided to tank? As fate would have it, I ran into an older colleague of mine who illustrated this point in a very personal way for me.

Dr. Ted was a mentor to me and had been very influential in my decision to pursue medicine when we met during my undergraduate years. A hardworking general surgeon with a keen eye for the market, Dr. Ted always had a quick anecdote about the performance of a particular stock he had bought or sold recently. We hadn't seen each other in years, but in early 2009 I paid a visit to his office. Then in his early seventies, he was still spry and sharp as ever, but he confessed that he had planned to retire the previous year.

Like everyone else who had had the bulk of their wealth tied to the stock market, he'd taken significant paper losses and didn't want to lock them in by selling. Instead, he decided to keep working, removing gallbladders, seeing patients, and taking overnight calls for an additional two and a half years until the market had recovered sufficiently for him.

Two and a half years is precious time no matter what age you are, but even more so when you are in your seventies. After a lifetime of working so hard and seeing such success, that certainly wasn't the way he had anticipated spending his golden years. Now, some might argue, and rightly so, that he should have begun shifting some money into less-risky assets as he neared retirement. Nonetheless, his situation powerfully illustrated the life-altering consequences of a sudden, uncontrollable loss of wealth that was possible with traditional equities. That was a big wake-up call for me. Not long after, I started wondering what other opportunities there might be that could provide more consistent returns, with risk uncorrelated to the stock market. And I went looking for them.

The following chapters represent more than three years of exploration, learning, and experiences in the world of what are known as alternative investments. Alternative investments, broadly defined, are anything other than the traditional paper assets of stocks, bonds, money market accounts, and CDs with which we are all familiar. The world of alternative investments is vast with opportunities to fit literally any budget, return potential, risk tolerance, or investment objective. Consequently, it was important for me to come up with criteria by which to evaluate and potentially participate in certain asset classes.

Number one, I wanted high yield, generally defined as at least double the official inflation rate. I therefore chose 5 percent annual returns as my minimum threshold. In reality, most have a track record of returns in the high single-digit to low double-digit range (8 to 12 percent). Number two, I wanted risk that was uncorrelated with the equities market, meaning the next time stocks took another precipitous decline, my investments wouldn't necessarily go down in parallel.

This book represents a distillation of all the many hours of podcasts, conferences, videos, and phone calls that I have engaged in over the past three years in order to learn about and ultimately participate in a number of alternative investments that fit these criteria.

Some of them are longstanding asset classes that you may be somewhat familiar with, such as rental properties and private mortgage lending. Others are newer, emerging areas that are on the technological and regulatory cutting edge of finance, including peer-to-peer lending and real estate crowdfunding. Some require as little as twenty-five dollars to get started, others $25,000 or more. Some require assembling a local network, while others are accessible with just a few taps on your smartphone.

Now, to be clear, I am not an investment professional, so none of the content here should be taken as formal advice, and likewise when it comes to taxation and business issues. You need to consult with your CPA and attorney in those matters. My day job is that of a cancer doctor. That may be off-putting to some of you. After all, I am not a credentialed expert in the arena of finance and investing. However, I know there is a group of you that is likely to find it refreshing to hear the voice of someone who is not an insider in this arena and, perhaps most importantly, has no financial product to sell you. I can share with you my journey from being a traditional investor in paper assets to becoming someone who has wholeheartedly embraced alternatives.

Patients often confront me with questions about alternative treatments, as they understandably want to avoid the unpleasant side effects associated with traditional radiation and chemotherapy. While very little of what they ask about has any proven benefit, I certainly understand the motivation. Fortunately, in the world of investments, there are many alternatives that "work," meaning they can deliver real returns in the 8 to 12 percent range or more, mimicking the historic returns of the stock market but without the volatile downswings or prolonged flat periods.

In all instances, I will endeavor to give you a clear understanding of how the investments work and how they have performed for me. Additionally, I will highlight useful online resources along with both my due diligence practices and pitfalls to watch out for.

Your Guide to Alternative Investments

In the chapters that follow, the specific types of investments include:

Peer lending: Earn healthy returns acting as a banker to creditworthy people or businesses.

Student loan investing: Refinance student loans to help graduates better manage their debt with lower payments while making a safe return that is still much higher than a savings account.

Private mortgage lending: Lend on fix-and-flip or buy-and-hold properties to make double-digit returns secured by real estate.

Real estate crowdfunding: In a technological twist, it is now possible to pool money from many individuals for private real estate lending. Crowdfunding isn't just for your college roommate's indie film passion project anymore. Now it's an all-access pass to get in on great real estate investments all over the country for less money.

Turnkey rental property: Income-producing property is one of the most time-tested asset classes in history and deserves a serious look for anyone looking to build long-term wealth. The perceived time and management requirements hold many people back from exploring ownership. There are companies devoted to making the ownership experience hassle free whether your property is down the street or across the country.

Distressed mortgage notes: Make a profit while doing social good. Specialty hedge funds purchase huge pools of delinquent mortgages at steep discounts from banks. They then work with the homeowners to work out a financial solution that is affordable and still produces an attractive return for investors.

In the next chapter, you'll learn about the exciting things going on in online peer-to-peer lending. Private investors like you and me are giving the big banks a run for their money when it comes to refinancing credit card debt for creditworthy borrowers—and those investors are making a nice return in the process.

Chapter 2

Peer-to-Peer Lending

Peer-to-Peer Lending

The Father of Online Peer Lending

The consumer credit sector is a massive $3 trillion market, and much of this consumption is financed with credit cards. As a rule, credit cards are expensive, with an average annual percentage rate of 17 percent, which can easily be much higher. On the other hand, the Federal Reserve has maintained historically low interest rates on bank savings accounts for close to a decade, struggling to average a return of 1 percent.

Bearing this in mind, back in 2006, French Internet entrepreneur Renaud Laplanche seized upon what would become a revolutionary idea in investing—while looking through his mail. First, he opened up his credit card statement and noted—with some displeasure, no doubt—that he was being charged an interest rate of 18 percent on what he owed. Next, he happened to look at his bank statement. On the breakdown for his savings account, he saw that he was earning an interest rate of just 1 percent.

Flashing back between those two interest rates, a light bulb went on in his head. "Look," he thought. "Why can't I take some of the money from my savings, which is earning nothing there, and refinance someone else's high-interest-rate credit card debt?" If he and the borrower could meet somewhere in the middle of that 17 percent spread, he could lower that person's credit card payments and significantly raise the passive rate of return on his savings. And why couldn't that work on a much bigger scale? All sorts of people might be interested in entering into deals like that.

He was right. Plenty of people thought that sounded like a much better way to earn a return on their savings. That's how online peer-to-peer lending was born. Essentially, investors who make peer-to-peer loans are acting as bankers for individual borrowers, allowing them to refinance their credit card debt at a lower rate and saving them money. In turn, the investor gets a return on his or her investment.

In this chapter, I cover how peer-to-peer lending works, as well as online resources you can use to learn more before you invest. You'll also find guidelines for success and how to perform due diligence on specific opportunities. The focus here will be on Lending Club, the largest and most established of the peer-to-peer platforms.

Once you see how easy it is to make a relatively safe, consistent return this way, you too may start to seriously consider this emerging asset class.

Peer-to-peer, along with peer-to-business lending and real estate crowdfunding, are all examples of online financial technology platforms that have the following common features:

Due diligence: The platforms themselves generally perform due diligence on the opportunity, in that there are specific criteria to be met before it can be listed. Additionally, they provide easy-to-use tools to perform a more detailed analysis by the investor prior to committing money.

Marketplace: The platforms conveniently bring together buyers and vetted sellers.

Small capital requirements: Many follow the crowdfunding model that allows investment with relatively small sums of money compared with traditional methods of participating in these assets.

Digital document execution: Mortgages, promissory notes, management agreements, and more can all be signed electronically.

How It Works

Laplanche launched Lending Club on three important pillars of the new platforms: marketplace, due diligence, and small capital requirements. On one side of the ledger are the borrowers. In order to qualify, you must have a minimum FICO score of 620, verifiable employment for one year, and a maximum debt-to income ratio of 40 percent. That said, the typical borrower's profile is actually much better than these minimum standards. The average FICO score is 699, with an income of $71,000 (US median $52,000) and a debt-to-income ratio of 17 percent. The maximum loan size one can qualify for is $35,000 for an either three- or five-year duration.

The platform goes a step further by performing a more detailed analysis of the borrower's creditworthiness, scrutinizing additional data such as homeowner status and length of employment. All of these data points are ultimately distilled into a letter grade of A to G, corresponding to the interest rate a borrower will pay for his or her loan, or "note," as this is often referred to. A-rated borrowers receive rates in the 5 percent to 6 percent range, while the worst of G borrowers can see rates north of 20 percent.

Under the "Manual Investing" tab, you can search for new loans and sort them by borrower risk, loan purpose, and duration, among other criteria.

There is a significant depth of additional information about the individual borrowers provided to potential investors on peer-to-peer lending platforms. If you want, you can browse and click on a borrower's profile and see his or her job title, monthly income, credit report, and homeowner status. Alternately, you can use the site's filter tabs and select a group of borrowers with the specific characteristics you're looking for. This is what I typically do, because it saves time. In a nutshell, all of this due diligence by the platform makes it easy for investors to quickly make a decision about which type of borrower they are comfortable lending to.

The other key feature of peer-to-peer lending is that the investors are able—and in fact encouraged—to loan no more than the site's minimum of twenty-five dollars to any individual borrower. In effect, the investors wind up with a portfolio of dozens or hundreds of micro loans to many individuals. This minimizes the impact of defaults on any one particular loan and is a key protection strategy. In turn, the borrowers receive a fairly quick and efficient crowdfunded loan.

Best Practices

Personally, I treat my Lending Club account as a new type of savings account (i.e., I am relatively conservative, in that I limit my investments to the least risky borrowers to minimize defaults). To this end, I typically choose people who have a 700+ credit score and who make at least $6,000 per month. I also choose only three-year-period notes, instead of the five-year ones, but that doesn't always necessarily mean that my money is going to be locked up for that full three-year period. By choosing people with a high income level and good credit histories, I've had situations occur where my borrowers have paid off their loans ahead of schedule—sometimes in less than a year.

Here is an example of the account summary page you would first see when logging on to your club account. We see this person's annual return is in the 7 to 10 percent range typical for most investors with a well-diversified portfolio of loans on the platform.

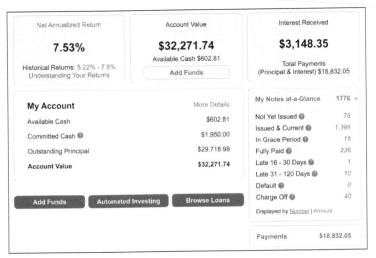

If you were to do a Web search for peer-to-peer lending strategies, you would find a wealth of websites, blogs, and commentaries about the specific filters people use and the results they have been able to attain. A personal favorite of mine is Lend Academy, where owner Peter Renton shares his strategy and historic returns—candidly and in detail—from over a number of years. If, however, a more passive experience is desired, the site can automatically invest on your behalf in loan grades you preselect. It is also worth noting Lending Club can accommodate IRA money, providing a creative way to diversify your retirement funds and enjoy some tax benefits on your returns.

Risks

The downside to peer-to-peer lending is that these are ultimately non-secured loans, and so there will be an inevitable number of defaults, even among the A-rated borrowers. Many sites have collections processes in place but caution investors on the low likelihood of meaningful recovery if a borrower defaults. So it's important to understand from the outset that there's going to be some loss with little recourse. It is for this reason, again, that Lending Club strongly recommends that you loan no more than the site's minimum of twenty-five dollars to any individual borrower.

The nice thing about Lending Club in particular is that the site has been around sufficiently long enough (since 2007) to establish a track record of actual delinquency rates versus those predicted for each letter grade. Lending Club has found that for those investors who are at the minimum recommended level of diversification (i.e., four hundred loans), the predicted versus actual returns and delinquencies correlate very well. Additionally, no investor with this portfolio size has ever experienced a negative overall return on the site.

The other downside is that there's not much liquidity in these loans. For example, say you invested in a number of three-year loans, and they have been performing as expected for the first six months with regular payments. If, for whatever reason, you needed to get your original investment back early, your options are very limited. Unlike the stock market, where you can buy and sell virtually instantly, there is no robust secondary market to sell peer-to-peer loans. There are some developing, but currently these are small and cannot handle the rapidly growing volume of peer-to-peer notes. Now, I have had several borrowers pay back their notes in full early, but this is unpredictable, so I count on holding the note for the stated duration when I make an investment through this platform.

On a macroeconomic level, another potential risk with peer-to-peer lending is that no one is quite sure to what degree we would see a spike in delinquencies should the economy take another significant downturn. We can make some inferences from looking at traditional credit card data, but overall, the asset class of peer-to-peer lending is still just too new to make a reliable judgment here.

Lastly, there is platform risk, or the risk of the platform itself going out of business. The sites make their money by taking a fee, typically 1 percent of the investor return, and thus far this business model is working well. In the event the platforms were to go bankrupt, however, they have in place what are termed "back-up servicers" that would take over the vital marketplace functions in order to protect both the borrowers and the investors. Lending Club went public with a very well-received IPO in December 2014, significantly decreasing bankruptcy risk for this particular platform and bolstering investor confidence for the sector as a whole.

How to Get Started

Currently, Lending Club is available in forty-one states, and that number continues to grow. Except for in California, there is no minimum income requirement to get started as an investor. So the vast majority of US investors can open an account with as little as twenty-five dollars. You can visit LendingClub.com for more information about specific requirements for investors based on your state of residence.

Once you've started making peer-to-peer loans, it's important to keep up to date on your account. I usually check my account via my smartphone twice per week. Once I log in, I'm greeted with a summary screen reflecting new principal and interest payments that have come in. Next, I go to the "Manual Investing" tab, which brings up newly listed notes available for investment. While you can select loans on an individual basis, I use the saved filter feature to quickly find those notes that meet my borrower criteria with respect to income, credit score, and other criteria. Once selected, the default of twenty-five dollars populates into the amount field, and I can adjust it upwards if desired. Then I just hit "Confirm," and I'm done.

Typically, this entire process takes less than five minutes, and it is very satisfying to see your account grow over time through constant reinvestment of interest profits. My returns have been in the 7 percent range over the two years I have been investing with Lending Club, which is consistent with the projections for my typical borrower profile. As my comfort level grows, I plan on gradually increasing my risk tolerance to aim for 9 percent to 10 percent returns.

Online Resources

Many peer-to-peer lending platforms are emerging—far too many to list here. That said, some notable players include the following:

- **Lending Club (LendingClub.com)**

  Launched in 2007, Lending Club is the oldest and largest peer-lending platform. As I've discussed, it has a very good track record. Plus, when the company went public in December 2014, it raised nearly $900 million, making it the largest US tech industry IPO of that year. Since then, it has branched off into other areas of lending—home improvement, small business—but 70 percent of all loans made through the platform are still going to refinancing high-interest credit cards or other high-interest lines of credit. Lending Club's advantages over its competitors include a very intuitive user interface on its website and a larger volume of loans, making it an easy and highly reliable way to deploy your capital.

- **Prosper (Prosper.com)**

  While I particularly like Lending Club, the next biggest player in the peer-to-peer lending market is Prosper. Prosper offers loans to borrowers at a slightly lower end of the credit spectrum, with minimum FICO scores of 640 and, hence, slightly higher returns if you are comfortable with the risk. Fundamentally, it offers the same product as Lending Club. The difference is that Lending Club is bigger and better capitalized, which suggests less platform risk.

- **Lending Club's Folio FN Trading Platform (LendingClub.com/foliofn/)**

  Folio FN is a partner with Lending Club that allows investors to sell off some of their Lending Club loans prior to maturity. Folio FN's goal is to provide a thriving secondary market to add liquidity to peer-to-peer investments. Personally, I have not had the need to use this platform, but knowing that it exists and is growing at a rapid pace is worth keeping in mind.

Once you get comfortable enough with the idea of peer lending that you start looking at platforms, I recommend that you go with one that's been around for a minimum of five or six years, so you can see how loans have performed historically on that particular site.

The Future of Banking as We Know It?

The amount of business currently being done on peer-lending platforms is growing rapidly. When Lending Club first launched, it took five years to loan out a total of $1 billion. But it loaned out $1 billion in the single calendar year of 2012 alone. Now it does $1 billion of loans every few months. As more people catch on, these numbers have been going up exponentially, and they are likely to continue to rise.

To put things into perspective, when you look at the entire credit market, the business happening on these platforms today is still just a small blip. Even so, as they continue to expand, peer-lending platforms have the potential to completely revolutionize the credit lending industry as we know it. More and more, we'll see people lending each other money, rather than our historical reliance on loans from big institutions. Being in on the ground floor of that is exciting.

Now that you've learned the basics about how peer-to peer lending works, we'll turn our attention to a similar alternative investment: peer-to-business lending, which is already significantly and positively influencing the ability of small businesses to survive and thrive.

Chapter 3

Peer-to-Business Lending

The Challenge of Funding Small Businesses in Today's Market

If you are like me, you probably didn't start out in life having a working knowledge of the various types and numbers of business entities in the United States. A few definitions and numbers will put things into a necessary context for understanding this chapter.

According to the US Chamber of Commerce, a big business is defined as one that has more than five hundred employees. Only nineteen thousand businesses worldwide fall into this category, and we all know many of their names. These are the Coca-Colas, McDonald's, and Disneys of the world.

A small business is therefore any that has fewer than five hundred employees. There are approximately twenty-eight million of these in the United States, where small businesses comprise 99.7 percent of the entire business landscape. Three-fourths of these entities are solo operations with no employees. So the remaining quarter contains what we call "neighborhood businesses," usually employing between two and twenty people.

Think about places you frequent—the local restaurants or cafés, dry cleaners, and auto repair centers. They provide not only a significant economic function but also an important social function vital to any stable community. For this reason, small businesses are the focus of this chapter.

If consumer spending is a primary pillar of the American economy, small or neighborhood business is certainly an important consideration. Some relevant stats worth taking note of include the following:

Small businesses

- Have increased in number by 49 percent since 1982
- Account for 54 percent of all US sales
- Provide 55 percent of all jobs and have provided 66 percent of all net new jobs since the 1970s
- Occupy approximately 40 percent of all commercial real estate space, to the tune of thirty billion square feet
- Have added eight million new jobs since 1990, as big businesses *eliminated* four million jobs

With this backdrop, one would assume the traditional banking sector would have seen an expanding role in financing this growth in recent years. But this is not the case.

In fact, over the last two decades, the number of short-term loans made to small businesses from traditional lending institutions has fallen drastically.

This is in part because, in the wake of the financial crisis, many of the smaller banks that used to service these businesses have simply gone out of business. The number of small banks (defined as those having $10 billion or less in assets) declined 27 percent from 2000 to 2014. Simultaneously, the ranks of large banks increased 32 percent over this time.

According to Brendan Ross, president of Direct Lending Investments and a pioneer in the peer-to-business space, in 1998, loans of under $1 million to small businesses represented about half of all bank loans. Today, that number stands closer to 28 percent.

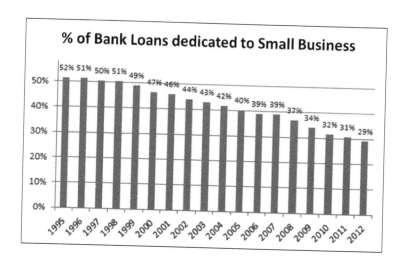

The larger banks don't provide these loans because it is unprofitable for them to do so.

All lenders charge a percentage of the loan as a fee; this constitutes their profit. For this reason, the big banks concentrate on loans of a million dollars and up, because they require the same amount of work to originate as the smaller loans do. Even the Small Business Administration (SBA) caters to entities on the larger end of the spectrum, when you consider that the size of its average loan is $371,000.

It is also important to remember that, increasingly, many small businesses are service oriented, and thus often have characteristics big banks don't like from an underwriting perspective. These include having seasonal or uneven earnings, and lacking ownership of significant amounts of physical capital to serve as collateral.

Traditional financing alternatives that service small businesses have included very expensive merchant cash-advance companies. These entities can routinely charge annual interest rates north of 35 percent and even occasionally flirt with triple digits!

Unfortunately, this has led to a significant spike in interest rates for small-business loans from traditional lenders as well, and that puts business owners in a bad situation.

Small neighborhood businesses that provide jobs to local residents often need loans and lines of credit in the range of $50,000 to $250,000.

What if one of these businesses needs a small, short-term

loan so it can pay its vendors? Or to buy much-needed new equipment that's just not in the budget for another few months?

While this is understandably frustrating to small-business owners, the lack of small banks able and willing to make these kinds of loans to small businesses has left a void for technologically innovative lenders to fill.

Peer-to-business lending works quite a lot like peer-to-peer lending, only in this case, you are acting as a banker to a business rather than an individual. Attractive returns in the 12 percent to 24 percent range are routinely possible, while still providing capital at a cheaper rate than other financing options.

In this chapter, you'll learn about what you need to get started in peer-to-business lending, as well as preferred online resources, tips for due diligence, and best practices using some examples from my own investment history in this market.

How It Works

In our discussion of peer-to-business lending, I will focus on two particular platforms: Funding Circle and P2Binvestor. Both offer features that share many parallels with Lending Club, including marketplace, due diligence, and small capital requirements.

Funding Circle provides loans for the full spectrum

of business activities, including payroll, new equipment, marketing, and new hires. P2Binvestor, on the other hand, focuses specifically on factoring loans. Depending on the nature of the business, there can be a long time gap between services being rendered and the company actually getting paid. Factoring loans provide the needed capital to fill in that gap and meet ongoing expenses.

Which types of neighborhood businesses are eligible? It is important to realize that lending to a small business in general is inherently risky. According to the US Bureau of Labor Statistics, only about half of all new establishments survive five years or more, and about one-third survive ten years or more.

In order to mitigate against these risks, platforms have a number of criteria that businesses must meet prior to receiving an investor loan.

For example, P2Binvestor strictly forbids startups. Its average business is typically at least seven years old, with revenue in the $500,000 to $2 million annual range and a daily cash flow of at least $20,000. Sometimes, access to the business's bank account or accounting software is required as a real-time method of monitoring the borrower's financial status. P2Binvestor also requires automated electronic repayments on a weekly or even daily basis.

In addition, the principal owner is usually required to have excellent credit, with a FICO score of close to 700. The owner may also be required to sign a personal loan guarantee as an extra measure of security. (A personal guarantee is a legal pledge by the owner to make good on a business loan, even if it has to come from his or her personal assets.)

Another key distinguishing feature of the online peer-to-business lenders is digital submission of financial data during the underwriting process.

Even when there were more traditional lenders in the "pre-crisis" period, the process of getting a loan was burdensome from a time and logistics perspective. All of the required paper documentation had to be gathered together for an in-person submission to a bank officer, followed by a waiting period of several weeks before the potential borrower was ultimately informed of the bank's decision. The overall success rate was quite low, hovering around the 15 percent mark.

Now, thanks to the electronic submission capability of peer-to-business lending platforms, a loan decision can be made in a matter of days or even hours. Under many circumstances, this accelerated speed can be critical to the success of an entrepreneur.

The sites, in turn, provide detailed information to investors. At the touch of a button, you can drill down and look at a business's tax returns for the last three years, profit and loss statements, liabilities—essentially, everything you'd want to see before pulling the trigger on that investment.

This is similar to the types of analysis you could do

on a publicly traded company, where these kinds of data (particularly earnings) are readily available.

Like Lending Club, Funding Circle uses a letter grading system to categorize the level of risk for any individual business ranging from A to F, corresponding to investor returns between 5.5 percent and 23 percent.

Once approved, the loan is listed on the platform and funded by a network of investors. It's worth noting that average individual loan amounts for peer-to-business lending are much larger compared with peer-to-peer lending. The minimum investment for this kind of loan typically ranges from $500 to $1,000.

Browse marketplace

Loan title	Risk	Amount	Term	Rate	Time left	Amount left		Actions
Fitness Sports Club - 1/4/2015 Other services (except Public Administration), NY	A+	$375,000 23%	60 mo	10.49%	4 days	$288,411	$ Amount	Buy
Furniture Manufacturer - 12/31/2015 Manufacturing, CA	A	$300,000 41%	60 mo	12.69%	3 days	$178,418	$ Amount	Buy

How to Get Started

So who can invest?

If you want to participate on the specific platforms I've discussed in this chapter, you will need a minimum of $25,000 to $50,000. This is principally so that you, the investor, will be able to achieve the diversification needed, spreading your default risk among several loans.

Additionally, you need to be an accredited investor. According to the SEC, in order for an individual to qualify as an accredited investor, a person must accomplish at least one of the following:

1. Earn an individual income of more than $200,000 per year, or a joint (married) income of $300,000, in each of the last two years, and expect to reasonably maintain the same level of income

2. Have a net worth exceeding $1 million, either individually or jointly with his or her spouse

This is a large hurdle for many investors, but two things are worth bearing in mind. First, the SEC is working on rules to allow non-accredited investors to participate on these kinds of platforms. You can perform a Google search for "Title III of the JOBS Act" to monitor this situation. Second, and as mentioned previously, there are small-business lending opportunities on Lending Club that do not have the accreditation requirement.

Please keep in mind that this sector shares all of the default, platform, and liquidity risks as described in the previous chapter on peer-to-peer lending.

Best Practices Drilldown

Because the volume of business loans is much smaller than that of personal loans, peer-to-business platforms are very proactive when it comes to notifying you of new listings via email. You can expect to receive email updates of this nature once or twice per week. When I receive one of these emails, I can use the links embedded in it to navigate directly to the site's marketplace and can invest right from my phone in just a few minutes.

One example of a specific loan I'm participating in on Funding Circle is for an optometric practice. The total loan amount is $150,000, so the $1,000 I put in translates to 0.67 percent of that loan. And the interest rate I'm making on that is 18.49 percent annually over a three-year period.

This particular loan has been classified as a C-grade deal on a scale of A to F by Funding Circle's proprietary underwriting process. Based on my own (generally conservative) comfort level with risk, this is the highest level of risk I will take on in this space.

Funding Circle provides three years' worth of financials on each business, including profit and loss statements and balance sheets. This provides an excellent opportunity for an investor to do his or her own due diligence, which I recommend—especially when you're first getting started with a new platform.

While I initially performed a more granular analysis on each individual investment, over time I have become more comfortable with relying more on the platform's underwriting standards.

At this point, I simply don't invest in D–F loans, or any loan that has more than the minimum three-year duration. In other words, I invest only in businesses with good credit ratings, and on loans that will keep my money tied up for the shortest length of time possible. Currently, there is no secondary market for these securities, so I plan on holding them for the duration—although early payback is, again, possible.

After slightly more than a year on Funding Circle, my net returns have been a very satisfactory 14 percent.

Making an Impact with Local Small Businesses

It's important to remember that an estimated 70 percent of all jobs in this country are based on neighborhood businesses. They are truly the backbone of our economy, yet, as we've covered here, banks are increasingly skittish about small-business loans.

Compare that with the speed with which some of these fintech lending platforms can fund a small-business loan—usually within a week, and sometimes as quickly as *three days*. When you're a small-business owner who needs to pay rent and get payroll done, that time can mean the difference between success and going out of business.

In providing much-needed capital for these businesses, these new platforms are helping the economy to grow and giving investors like myself, who previously never had any money in this asset class, new access to valuable opportunities.

Now that you've become educated about the growing market and opportunities in peer-to-business lending, we're on to yet another exciting online lending category: real estate crowdfunding. Before we cover how it's done online, however, we need to get a firm handle on how it works offline, otherwise known as private mortgage lending.

Chapter 4

Private Mortgage Lending

No Banks Required

If you are like me, then for most of your adult life, you have associated a bank with all facets of real estate transactions—particularly for residential properties. It wasn't until recently that I discovered the considerable market for private real estate lending, sometimes referred to as hard money lending.

Private lending is simply when an individual, rather than an institution, puts up the money for a real estate venture. Real estate crowdfunding represents an emerging fintech-focused version of this longstanding form of financing, and it is covered in depth in the next chapter. However, traditional private lending is such a central component of real estate investing that it deserves a full chapter to itself.

In my experience, two main groups of people look for private money to use in taking control of a residential property. The first group is house flippers—people who buy, fix, and sell distressed properties for a profit. The second group is "buy and hold" investors—landlords who are seeking to put together a large portfolio of rental properties.

The ways in which these two groups use this private money from investors is very different, but the reason why they prefer getting it this way instead of from banks is the same: fast, easy access to capital when a good opportunity arises.

High-volume professional house flippers and investor landlords have networks of agents, wholesalers, probate attorneys, and others who provide them early or sometimes exclusive access to off-market properties. These can often be purchased at a significant discount with cash.

Additionally, there are plenty of instances where someone is particularly eager to sell due to the big four life-change reasons: death, divorce, job loss, or job change. Under circumstances such as these, the seller may already have the property listed at an attractive price, but if you can offer cash and close quickly (in under two weeks), you can often negotiate an even better price.

Contrast this with another prospective buyer who has to get a bank loan, which takes—on average—forty-five days.

In this chapter, I'll cover how to work with both house flippers and investor landlords in private lending arrangements, including what you need to get started, online resources, risks to consider, and best practices for success.

Private Lending to Fix-and-Flip Developers

The average house flipper can't go to a bank.

Banks, as a rule, do not lend on properties that need substantial rehabilitation and are not going to be occupied by the borrower. It is simply not part of their underwriting model.

In cases like these, the personal financial health of the borrowers/occupants is paramount—their FICO score, income, etc. A bank will make a loan on the appraised as-is value of the house, and it is likely to want the extra security of the borrower living in the house in order to make the loan in the first place.

Neither of these conditions is met with the typical house rehabilitation project. The property, by definition, needs substantial work to get it up to market value, and the flipper isn't going to live there.

In contrast, a private lender is essentially underwriting the financial merits of the house flip itself. If the gap between the purchase price and the after repair value (ARV) is large enough, the lender knows there is enough profit to pay the 10 percent to 18 percent interest rates typical on these types of loans.

Another key feature is the short duration of these loans, which are usually in the range of six to eighteen months. This is generally sufficient time to allow for the acquisition, rehab, marketing, and ultimate sale to a retail homebuyer. Keep in mind that, depending on the extent of repairs needed and overall market conditions, a flip can easily be accomplished in considerably less time than six months. Go back and peruse the numbers on those *Flip This House*–type shows of the early 2000s; you will notice that they were financed with private money at interest rates of 10 percent or greater.

A firm distinction between private lending and hard money lending is difficult to define, but generally speaking hard money lenders are more often small financial companies, rather than individuals, and charge loan origination fees or points. The points are typically an additional 1 percent to 3 percent of the loan value collected up front.

Risk for Fix-and-Flip Lending

As with any type of investment, private lending for house flips comes with some level of risk. In this section, I break down the big-ticket items to look at when considering a private lending investment in this arena.

Check the Numbers

One thing you can do to minimize risk when lending for this type of project is to make sure the rehab developer can deliver what he or she is promising on the particular deal you're being offered.

The way to verify this is to look closely at the developer's ARV estimation for the project. If that number has been correctly nailed, then it's relatively easy to work backwards to determine what you should pay to acquire that property.

Generally, the developer is looking to make a profit of 25 percent to 30 percent. For example, if it costs $65,000 to acquire a house, and the estimated repairs are going to cost another $35,000, the ideal selling price for the house post-rehab should be at least in the $120,000 to $130,000 range. But that means that the ARV has to actually be valued, at a minimum, in that range. You'll want to look at comparable sales in that market to make sure those numbers line up.

This formula serves as a good benchmark in determining the maximum amount you should pay for a rehab property. Plan to loan no more than about 65 percent of the property's ARV price.

That way, if the deal ultimately doesn't hit that ARV number, there's still some room to drop the resale price of the house. If that scenario comes to pass, it should be the rehabber whose profit suffers; you should at least still get your initial investment back.

Verify the Quality and Speed of the Work Crew

The other big thing to look into is verifying the timeliness and work quality of the actual rehab crew your developer works with. It's important to make sure he or she is using a reliable contractor—someone he or she has worked with before and developed a relationship with, so that the speed and work quality of that contractor is not in question.

In turn, the contractor should have an experienced and reliable crew, as well as a network of similarly qualified and vetted specialty subcontractors (e.g., plumbers and electricians). That chain of existing relationships breeds accountability and results in a better chance of the project moving along within the expected time frame.

Best Practices for Fix-and-Flip Lending

My average return on this kind of investment ranges from 12 percent to 14 percent, with a loan period of between six months and one year. It's worth mentioning that I have had a few situations where an additional month or two of extension has been necessary to sell the property.

Some private lenders don't require monthly payments, allowing the interest to accrue until the house sells. However, like many private lenders, I think that monthly payments provide recurring extra incentive to complete the project quickly.

Additionally, writing monthly payments into the deal adds another small layer of safety for me. If the project goes belly up or the flipper ends up being a fraud, heaven forbid, then at least I've been collecting some money throughout that time period.

I have had one project where I agreed to let the interest accrue or build up, to be paid out at the time the property sold. As luck would have it, that property sat on the market for an extended period of time and had to be discounted to the point where the rehabber took a loss and was only able to give me back my original capital.

A little over a year with no return on investment—that was a mistake I won't make again.

Private Lending to Investor Landlords

In order to better understand how private lending to investor landlords works, consider the following scenario. An investor landlord—let's call her Jane—decides to start building a rental empire. She gets a loan from a bank for the first property, putting 20 percent down. Then Jane puts a renter in that property and cash starts flowing.

"Great!" Jane thinks. "Now I'm ready for another rental." So she goes and gets another mortgage from the bank. Typically, she can do that a total of ten times (but sometimes only up to four). After that, the bank comes back and says, "Sorry. Even though you're current on all your loans, we're not willing to give you any more loans to buy rental properties."

The reason for this is because the banks turn around and sell Jane's mortgage notes to Fannie Mae or Freddie Mac. Both of those entities place limits on how many mortgages taken out by the same individual they will buy from a bank.

So if Jane's goal is to have more than ten rental

properties and have them all financed, she's going to hit this limit that banks artificially impose upon her—even if her portfolio is performing. So when it's time to get that eleventh rental property, she's either paying cash for it or has to find funding from another source.

Private Lending to Investor Landlords: How It Works

I have been able to routinely charge interest rates in the 10 percent to 12 percent range for a duration of one to two years on loans to investor landlords.

While certainly more expensive than traditional bank financing, this can still be a profitable deal for the landlord, provided that the target property is purchased at a good price relative to its rental income. Again, the ability to make all-cash offers to motivated sellers is a great way to source these properties.

So how do I get my money back at the end of the loan term with this kind of lending?

Once Jane gets a tenant in place and can show six to twelve months' worth of cash-flow history, she can then get a "portfolio" loan based on the reliable rental income and refinance through a bank to a lower interest rate.

Portfolio lenders, in contrast to larger traditional banks, are regional financial institutions that keep the loans they make on their books for the duration rather than selling them off to Fannie Mae/Freddie Mac. Consequently, they have less-strict criteria and are willing to finance multiple properties for the same owner—as long as the numbers all add up.

Portfolio lenders tend to be much more focused on the underlying performance of the assets—particularly the rental cash flow—and less on the financial status of the borrower. As such, in our scenario, there's a strong likelihood they would provide Jane a loan with a lower interest rate, allowing her to cash me out.

At that point, once she is ready to buy another rental property, the whole process can repeat itself. I know of landlords who have financed upwards of fifty rental homes with this method.

Risk for Rental Property Loans

One thing I always check off my list for each deal is that I am covered under the rehabber or landlord's insurance policy.

Because I'm acting as the primary mortgage or lien holder, I'm just as liable if a worker on a rehab crew or tenant has a slip-and-fall injury. The same principle applies if there's a fire and the whole house burns to the ground. Getting liability and fire insurance allows me to make sure I'm protected.

Best Practices for Rental Property Loans

Some of the best advice I can offer in this arena is to establish working relationships with investor landlords who have a track record of success in this vein—and stick with them.

The main two people I work with for this type of lending are a married couple who own about forty single-family rental houses in Jacksonville, Florida. Six of those forty rental properties are fully paid off, so they've got mortgages on the other thirty or so. For them, it has been an absolute necessity to get private money to fund the additional units they've added to their portfolio. I approached this situation as a portfolio lender would—by evaluating the performance of the assets.

A current appraisal showed there was equity (i.e., the houses were worth more than what was owed on them, and the regular rental payments were easily covering their outstanding debt, with cash flow to spare).

I also got a personal guarantee for an additional layer of safety. This is when the investor landlord signs a legal document pledging to make good on a business loan out of his or her personal assets if necessary.

How to Get Started in Private Lending

There is no way around it: traditional private lending requires a significant chunk of capital.

Even for very inexpensive homes (for both fix-and-flips and lending to investor landlords), you generally need a minimum of $25,000 and, typically, much more to fund the type of working-class-neighborhood houses I target.

Few of us have that kind of savings sitting around, but people have used a couple of common methods to raise the necessary capital. As with all new business endeavors, pooling money together from friends and family is a viable option. I have done this myself, offering to pay them a return of 8 percent, while reliably earning 12 percent or more on their borrowed funds. Resist the temptation to conduct handshake deals; instead, have formal agreements/promissory notes drawn up by an attorney.

A second and less well-known option is a self-directed IRA. For many of us, our retirement accounts represent the largest single source of savings we have. While a full discussion of self-directed IRAs is beyond the scope of this book, it should be noted that it is possible to use your retirement funds for real estate investing without compromising their tax-favored status.

Specialized companies or "custodians" are needed to set this up. I use a firm well known to real estate investors called EquityTrust.com, and its site has a wealth of information on the topic if you wish to learn more.

When it comes to finding reliable people to work with, traditional private lending is still a very offline, networking-intensive endeavor. I would start by asking around at your local Real Estate Investors Association chapter. The real professionals will have a reputation that can easily be validated by numerous people. Conversely, people with spotty reputations, part-timers, and newbies can also be identified and avoided in this way.

Real estate agents, lawyers, and bankers would also likely know who the very active flippers and landlords are in your city or community and, as such, can be another great resource.

You can even just Google "hard money lenders" and the name of your town to find active investors who can point you in the right direction. Alternatively, if you happen to know people who fix and flip properties or own rentals, you can develop those kinds of relationships over time in person.

Good places to start online to learn more include the following:

- **BiggerPockets.com**

  I love this site. I listen to its podcast in the morning while I'm on the treadmill or commuting. It ranks near the top of the real estate category in iTunes, and it's not hard to see why. There's a huge online community where people post regularly on all aspects of real estate investing. If you take the time to fully use this platform, it can teach you just about everything you need to get started.

- **American Association of Private Lenders (AAPL.com)**

  I particularly like this organization's YouTube channel, which you can find through the site. It offers a few free seminars and webinars that are great learning tools.

Now that you have an understanding of how traditional private lending works, let's see how real estate crowdfunding introduces some considerable technological twists to this longstanding alternative asset.

Chapter 5

Real Estate Investing Made Easy

It is predicted that, in 2016, crowdfunding will account for more funding than venture capital—exceeding more than $34 billion. This represents tremendous growth, from less than $1 billion in 2010. Most people these days have some basic familiarity with crowdfunding platforms such as Kickstarter and Indiegogo. These rewards-based sites offer consumers the chance to partially fund projects of interest to them. Get enough participants to chip in in exchange for perks or to pre-order your finished product, and you can get your project fully funded and off the ground.

Real estate crowdfunding applies this same revolutionary funding model to traditional equity and debt real estate deals. In short, crowdfunding allows a geographically diverse group of people to participate in a single project using relatively small amounts of money. Because it's not correlated with the stock market and is available to investors at a lower cost of entry, real estate crowdfunding is unique and in some respects safer to access than traditional offline investments. In my experience, returns have been in the range of 9 percent to 14 percent annually. That's comparable to the returns you'd stand to see on traditional real estate investment deals—and readily accessible online to anyone with a mobile device. Once you learn how much easier crowdfunding makes it to invest in real estate, you'll see why it has become my personal favorite of the fintech-enabled asset classes.

How It Works

Crowdfunding borrows elements from two established types of real estate financial structures: syndicates and real estate investment trusts (REITs).

Syndicates

Syndication is simply a fancy term for gathering money together from a large group of people to fund a real estate deal. Traditionally, syndicates have tended to fund large projects, such as an apartment complex or a commercial building. The minimum requirements to buy in to this kind of opportunity are typically in the $25,000 to $50,000 range. Besides this significant finan-cial hurdle, you also usually have to be connected socially somehow with the people involved in the project in order to invest.

REITs

REITs, on the other hand, are publicly traded entities that own large portfolios of real estate. These allow for much lower minimum investments, with shares of some being less than twenty dollars. In this kind of structure, your investment is spread across the whole portfolio rather than on an individual property. Due to their tax structure, REITs are required to pay out regular dividends. And because REITs are listed on the stock exchange, their value tends to go up and down with the stock market, regardless of how the underlying assets are performing.

The Crowdfunding Model

Compared with these traditional structures, crowdfunding uniquely marries a low minimum-investment requirement with the ability to invest in a single property. At the same time, it simplifies and expands access to real estate deals to more investors. Just like other types of fintech investing platforms covered in previous chapters, one of the principal value propositions here is due diligence. Real estate crowdfunding platforms vet their real estate entrepreneurs (commonly called sponsors), as well as the merits of the deal itself.

Each sponsor's track record is reviewed. As a rule, before being allowed on the crowdfunding site the sponsor must have an extensive and verifiable offline track record of several successful conventionally funded deals. Often, the site even gets a personal guarantee from the developer to insure the investment loan. These added layers of security mean greater safety for you and your money. Likewise, the platforms do considerable due diligence on each individual deal. Market analyses, comparable sales data, and third-party appraisals are reviewed to verify the financial merits of the project. All of this information is readily available to the prospective investor.

To review, even a modest "offline" house flip rehab project can exceed $100,000 or more. Traditionally, a rehabber would partner with a single private lender to finance these renovation costs over a six- to eighteen-month period. Typical return rates for this model are in the 10 percent to 18 percent range, with monthly interest payments to the lender until the property sells. Obviously, the number of people who can write that kind of check is limited. Alternatively, a rehabber could list his or her project on a crowdfunding site and get a number of people to contribute $5,000 or, on some platforms, as little as $1,000 to the loan. Once the total amount is raised, the funds are released to the developer minus a small fee to the platform.

In addition to debt deals, these platforms offer equity or partial ownership deals as well. Generally, equity deals pay a little less in terms of monthly cash flow compared with debt, but they often have greater returns over the typical three- to five-year hold period. A common equity scenario would be to acquire an underperforming apartment complex, gradually renovate it over time, and raise rents. The higher cash flows would allow for a cash-out refinance from a bank or an outright sale at an appreciated price. In either case, returns in excess of 20 percent annualized are routinely achievable when you account for some of the tax advantages available for equity investments.

Crowdfunding offers a full spectrum of asset classes to choose from, ranging from single-family homes to apartments, commercial office space, hotels, and even self-storage units. I have participated in just about each of these types. Going out and trying to hunt down opportunities like these on your own would take a huge investment of time. Additionally, your search would likely be hampered by whether deals like this were available in your local area, and whether you knew the right people who could get you access. The beauty of real estate crowdfunding is that online platforms eliminate these barriers, providing awareness of and access to specific deals, along with all the information you need to make a decision. Let's take a closer look at these platforms and what you need to begin investing.

How to Get Started

As I mentioned, one of the biggest benefits of this kind of investment is that it eliminates the high cost of entry to make an investment. You can get started on your first real estate crowdfunding deal with as little as $1,000 to $5,000, although some platforms require a minimum investment of at least $30,000 to $40,000 for higher-end opportunities. About 90 percent of sites do require you to be an accredited investor, but there are a few that don't. It is only a matter of time before these opportunities are available to anyone, once Regulation A+ of the JOBS Act is finalized. Platforms that have emerged as leaders in the field include the following:

- **PatchofLand.com**

  Focusing on debt deals with a period of one year, these projects tend to be clustered in a few select markets in which the organization has particular expertise. Yields have consistently been in the 11 percent to 12 percent range, similar to my experience with traditional private lending. The minimum investment per project is often $5,000.

- **RealtyMogul.com**

  This platform has both equity and debt offerings, from single-family homes to unique commercial ventures such as hotels and self-storage facilities. The minimums tend to be on the higher end of the spectrum, typically more than $25,000. One of the most high-profile projects in the industry was its successful funding of the Hard Rock Hotel in Palm Springs, California, in 2014.

- **Groundfloor.com**

  This is a unique site in two respects. First, it offers a very low minimum investment at $100. And second, it currently offers opportunities available to non-accredited investors in select states. Groundfloor focuses on debt projects and single-family homes.

One thing to keep in mind is that some of these platforms (PatchofLand.com, for instance) are balance sheet lenders. This means that when a developer comes to them with a good deal, they fund the project with money from their own coffers or balance sheet. Then they list the offering on their sites so that individual investors can buy them out of the project. Other sites don't work like this. Instead of putting their own money in first, they're a pure marketplace, matching investors' money with projects and taking a small cut for this service. Some observers feel that the balance sheet approach offers an extra incentive for the platform to perform better due diligence on projects compared with the marketplace model, but I don't think the industry is mature enough to determine that.

Now that you have a better sense of where to begin your real estate crowdfunding journey, let's explore some due diligence and best practices steps you should take to make sure you have your bases covered before investing.

Due Diligence and Best Practices

Just as with other types of fintech investing platforms, one of the principal value propositions here is due diligence. I already covered the way in which platforms in this arena perform due diligence steps for their investors. Additionally, some sites provide an open forum akin to a message board where an interactive Q&A occurs between either the platform's diligence team or the developers themselves. This can benefit all potential investors prior to committing to the project. I like to read through that discourse and see if the developer's responses line up with what he or she is promising. On occasion, this has been very helpful.

A common point emphasized by all of these sites is that they routinely turn down more than 90 percent of the projects presented to them. Maintaining this selectivity is a crucial anchor to the long-term viability of this model. Inevitably, some deals are not going to perform as expected, and there will be reduced returns or even losses. If the frequency of these events is small, however, investor trust will be preserved and this emerging capital-raising model can survive long term.

Personally, I have a strong penchant for short-term debt deals on single-family homes, because it is relatively easy to get a sense of the accuracy of the proposed sales price for this kind of deal. I'm counting on the developer being able to sell that house as my exit strategy, so avoiding inflated price projections is particularly important. The platforms will often provide convenient links to well-known third-party sites such as Zillow, and I will often use others such as Realtor.com as well. Over time, I've gotten more comfortable with certain platforms that I've used frequently with good results. Nonetheless, I also maximally diversify by contributing the investment minimum on any particular project. This lessens the impact on my overall portfolio should a project not perform as expected.

To help you get a sense of how this works, here's an example of a specific crowdfunding deal I participated in. It was a two-bed, one-bath, single-family home fix-and-flip in Charlotte, North Carolina. The rehabber was seeking a minimum investment per lender of $5,000. And that was over a twelve-month loan period, with an expected return of 13 percent.

Basic parameters of a single-family home crowdfunded fix-and-flip debt deal including interest rate, loan size, ARV, and duration.

I liked that the property was described as being in Charlotte's arts district and near downtown, because at that time I'd been hearing people speak highly of how that city was growing and developing. Most importantly, the ARV sales price lined up with many similarly sized properties in the neighborhood. Consistent with best practices in traditional private lending, I wanted the rehabber to have significant skin in the game by limiting my loan to value (LTV) to around 65 percent to 70 percent. In this particular deal, the total loan amount that the developer was seeking was 69 percent—right on target. This is the same principle that banks employ when they make a loan on a house. They want you to be able to put a minimum of 20 percent down, so they know you have some skin in the game.

Monthly interest payments detailed in the "my investments" section of my account. A total of $474.87 in interest was earned over the life of the loan with the original principal paid back upon sale of the house.

Oct 01, 2014	Interest	September, 2014	Rehab in Charlotte's Art District (████████ Charlotte, NC 28205)	$34.31		▶ Expand
Nov 01, 2014	Interest	October, 2014	Rehab in Charlotte's Art District (████████ Charlotte, NC 28205)	$55.97		▶ Expand
Dec 01, 2014	Interest	November, 2014	Rehab in Charlotte's Art District (████████ Charlotte, NC 28205)	$54.17		▶ Expand
Jan 01, 2015	Interest	December, 2014	Rehab in Charlotte's Art District (████████ Charlotte, NC 28205)	$55.97		▶ Expand
Feb 01, 2015	Interest	January, 2015	Rehab in Charlotte's Art District (████████ Charlotte, NC 28205)	$55.97		▶ Expand
Mar 01, 2016	Interest	February, 2015	Rehab in Charlotte's Art District (████████ Charlotte, NC 28205)	$50.56		▶ Expand
Apr 01, 2016	Interest	March, 2015	Rehab in Charlotte's Art District (████████ Charlotte, NC 28205)	$55.97		▶ Expand
May 01, 2017	Interest	April, 2015	Rehab in Charlotte's Art District (████████ Charlotte, NC 28205)	$54.17		▶ Expand
Jun 01, 2015	Interest	May, 2015	Rehab in Charlotte's Art District (████████ Charlotte, NC 28205)	$54.17		▶ Expand
Jun 03, 2015	Interest	May, 2015	Rehab in Charlotte's Art District (████████ Charlotte, NC 28205)	$3.81		▶ Expand
Total				$474.87		▶ Expand All

A total of $474.87 in interest was earned over the ten-month span of the loan with the original $5,000 principal returned upon sale of the property. I was then free to invest in another opportunity on the website and keep my money at work if desired.

Exploit Tax Advantages

On debt deals, there are no particular tax advantages compared with doing the same kind of deal offline. If you use regular, after-tax money, you will be taxed on the interest you make as ordinary income. Most of these sites are set up so that you can use self-directed IRA retirement money, which provides the usual tax advantages. On equity deals, though, you receive the same tax write-off benefits you get in similar traditional offline deals. This includes depreciation, which can mean significant tax savings, particularly on bigger projects such as a large apartment complex.

Taking Root in Real Estate

The ability to participate in individual real estate investments with relatively small capital requirements via crowdfunding is an exciting development in alternative investing. Using technology to overcome the traditional barriers to this asset class offers the potential to truly democratize real estate finance.

Chapter 6

Distressed Mortgage Notes

The Root of the Problem

By now, I think we have a pretty good understanding of what brought about the mortgage meltdown of 2008, which nearly turned into a full-blown financial crisis. In the years leading up to the downturn, banks greatly relaxed their lending standards, providing increasingly risky mortgages to a new crop of customers. Many unsophisticated borrowers found themselves with access to a dizzying array of new products, including adjustable rate loans with monthly payments that greatly increased after an initial teaser period. Coupled with the fact that many customers were able to qualify with little documentation of income or assets, it is no surprise that the number of foreclosures exploded. Even people with bad credit could qualify as subprime borrowers. Home prices were falsely inflated, based not on the market fundamentals of actual demand for housing, but on the speculation that the prices would continue to rise.

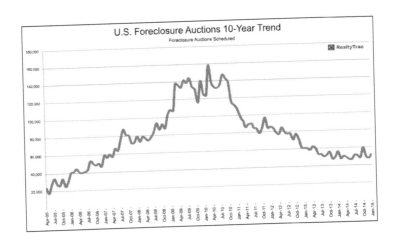

On the back end of this process were the large Wall Street banks, which eagerly bought these newly issued loans and packaged them together into a relatively new kind of financial product called a mortgage-backed security (MBS). Essentially functioning as a bond, mortgage-backed securities were sold in part to big institutional investors, such as pension funds, and insured against default by some of the largest insurance companies in the world, such as AIG. Once a sufficient number of borrowers began to default on their mortgage obligations, the whole house of cards fell apart, taking down some of the most recognized names in all of finance. Countrywide, Bear Stearns, and most notably Lehman Brothers, in the largest corporate bankruptcy in US history, were wiped out. Even larger entities such as AIG were poised to collapse and take down the entire US and, by extension, global financial system.

Nearly a trillion dollars of taxpayer money was used as a government bailout to keep these institutions, deemed "too big to fail," afloat. On a side note, the 2015 feature-length movie *The Big Short* was all about how an astute team of investors, led by a physician no less, figured out how to bet against the MBS market, turning themselves into billionaires in the process!

Without their Wall Street buyers on the back end, local banks continue to deal with a large volume of non-performing or distressed mortgages, generally defined as no payments for at least ninety days. And in some cases, the mortgages have been delinquent for years. This is because the legal and regulatory frameworks governing the foreclosure process are backlogged. We see this as a steady stream of bank-owned property listings of short sales, pre-foreclosures, and auction inventory.

At the time of this writing, the national average time to complete a foreclosure is approximately six hundred days and can easily exceed a thousand days or more in what are known as judicial states. Judicial states require court involvement at each step of the foreclosure, which greatly prolongs the process. Although they account for approximately 42 percent of all active mortgages, some 70 percent of loans in foreclosure are in these states. The states with the highest number of average days past due for loans in foreclosure are all judicial states: New York and Hawaii are each above 1,300 days, while New Jersey and Florida both top 1,200 days.

All the while, these bad loans on the books have significant negative consequences for the banks.

Banks make money by lending money. For every non-performing note held on a bank's balance sheet, the bank is required to hold reserve funds, which means it has less money available to lend. Additionally, there is the property itself to worry about. While many of these properties are occupied by the delinquent borrowers and therefore presumably being maintained to a livable standard, there are many other properties that have been abandoned. In order to protect the collateral for their loan, banks are reluctantly drawn into the property management business, incurring costs for trash removal, repairs, and lawn care, to name a few.

With these facts as a backdrop, you might imagine that if there were an expeditious way to get these bad loans off the books, it would be very attractive to banks. Enter institutional "note buyers." These are specialty hedge funds that raise money from investors and use those funds to buy large pools of distressed mortgages from banks. Owing to the volume and speed of the purchases, banks are willing to sell the non-performing notes at a fraction of the remaining loan value, referred to as the unpaid principal balance or UPB. Discounts of 30 percent or more can be common on first mortgages, while discount rates can be as high as

80 percent on riskier second mortgages. If you have never heard of distressed mortgage note investing, don't feel bad. With rare exceptions, banks don't sell small volumes of notes to individual investors.

Multiple Exit Strategies

Once the note buyer has possession of it, the mortgage represents a potentially very valuable asset with multiple profitable exit strategies. I say potentially because there is still work that must be done to realize an investment return. The note buyer can modify the original terms of the loan, creating a new affordable monthly payment more in line with the borrower's current economic situation. If that is not possible, other options include short sales, deed in lieu, or proceeding through the foreclosure process.

Hedge funds often have a preferred exit strategy. For instance, the particular funds I have invested in have neighborhood preservation and stability as a core mission. Therefore, they prefer to acquire occupied properties and do loan modifications to get the note re-performing and keep the borrower in the home long term. Because the mortgage was acquired at such an attractive price, there is often plenty of room to slash the monthly payment to less than half of its original amount and still make an attractive return. The note can be held as a cash-flowing asset or, after a period of regular payments has been established, sold off to another investor at a profit.

Other note companies like abandoned houses, which are much more likely to go through the foreclosure process and hence be repossessed. The companies can then renovate the property themselves into a long-term rental or retail sale, or quickly flip it "as is" to a real estate entrepreneur who will eventually do the same.

Still others might gravitate to the deed in lieu of foreclosure approach, whereby the borrowers are persuaded to voluntarily relinquish their ownership interest (deed) in the property to the lender as an expeditious way to avoid the foreclosure process.

Online Resources

So how do I participate in the distressed mortgage arena? As mentioned, I can't go down to my local bank, ask to look over its bad loans, and cherry pick an individual note for purchase. I have to go through either a note company or a specialized broker. Here are two companies I have been with for a couple of years and have been very satisfied with.

- **PPR Note Company**

  PPR stands for Partners for Payment Relief, and as the name suggests, PPR's focus is on loan modification leading to lower, sustainable monthly payments. Run by Dave Van Horn, PPR has been in business for more than ten years, raising specialty funds that offer investor returns in the low double-digit range annually with monthly recurring payments. You have to be accredited to participate, and the investment minimum is $10,000.00 with a three-year commitment. Dave writes extensively, with his blogs often featured on some of the most heavily trafficked real estate investment sites. PPR also regularly sells individual re-performing notes, with fund investors having preferential first access. For the entrepreneur who wants a more active experience, PPR Academy equips you with the knowledge necessary to source, evaluate, and modify notes on your own.

- **AHP**

  American Homeowner Preservation (AHP) leaves no ambiguity as to what its preferred exit strategy is. Similar to PPR, AHP wants to keep homeowners in place with loan modifications and has a special focus on properties in low-income neighborhoods hit particularly hard by the financial crisis. Jorge Newberry and the team at AHP believe in the 99 percent helping the 99 percent and have constructed a fund that anyone can participate in. Currently, AHP offers a 12 percent annual return with a very low minimum investment of $100.00—unheard of for this asset class! As an extra attractive feature, there is a high degree of liquidity, meaning you can get your original capital back upon request.

I should also mention that both funds can accommodate retirement funds if you have a self-directed IRA account. The high returns coupled with the tax advantage of a qualified account can be a potent combination for long-term wealth building.

When companies like AHP and PPR execute their preferred strategy, it truly is a win–win–win situation. Homeowners have affordable payments, and the note buyers make an attractive return that is then passed down to the investor.

Maybe some of you are wondering why banks don't do similar types of loan modifications and keep those new payments flowing their way. Well, in their defense, the loan modification process can be pretty time and labor intensive, requiring more personnel than a typical bank has on staff. A timeframe of several weeks to a few months is not uncommon to craft a suitable individual loan modification. Another key point to remember as well is that despite the surge in bad loans from the mortgage crisis, such loans still make up only a very small percentage of a bank's overall mortgage portfolio. So even if the banks wanted to make these kinds of loan modifications, logistically and economically it really doesn't make sense for them.

- **The Distressed Property Investing Group on LinkedIn**

  www.linkedin.com/topic/distressed-property

  This is an online meeting place for note company CEOs, brokers, and investors full of high-level conversation about the business. It is a great way to network and keep up on the latest developments.

Due Diligence/Pitfalls

As with any investment, there are some precautions one must take in order to avoid some potentially serious downsides with notes. Many of the specific risks mentioned here can be largely mitigated against by being diversified in a note fund as opposed to an individual note.

Property value: A home could have gone through such an extensive period of vacancy, neglect, and vandalism that the property is worth less than even the significant discount price paid for the note. When you consider the fact that many of the mortgages purchased are geographically spread out, having some reliable "boots on the ground" to assess the physical property can be crucial.

Bankruptcy: Not only can this greatly prolong an already lengthy foreclosure process, but it is possible that the homeowner may be able to legally discharge the mortgage debt, thereby eliminating the possibility of getting the note to re-perform.

Title issues: While it is generally easy to see major liens such as property taxes, which are recorded at the county office, it's possible there could be a host of other less well-disclosed liens on the property, such as from unpaid contractors or homeowners associations fees. An encumbrance and occupancy report can be ordered at extra expense to determine the status of all outstanding debts associated with the property.

This is by no means a comprehensive list, but it just illustrates the potential complexities that have to be navigated when dealing with individual notes. Certainly, the returns can be significantly higher, but as an investor desiring a passive experience, I am happy to participate in a fund and leave these potential headaches to the pros.

Note Workout Example

While I hope you have a good understanding of the basics of distressed note investing, nothing beats an actual real-life case study to illustrate how it works. This was sent to me from one of the note companies I used to invest with.

The fair market value of the house was $120,000, with a primary or first mortgage that had current payments and a balance of $114,000. In this example, the distressed note was a second mortgage, which is usually a home equity line of credit that many homeowners use for various repairs or enhancements to their property. The unpaid principal balance (UPB) of this distressed second mortgage was $53,799.62 and was acquired by the note company for $10,850, representing an approximately 80 percent discount off of the UPB.

In exchange for a discounted lump sum of $6,291 applied to the arrears and back payments, the note company was willing to issue a new thirty-year second mortgage with a favorable 3 percent interest rate. This translated into a very manageable monthly obligation of $408.11, which was nearly half the amount of the borrower's previous monthly payment.

You might be asking, how did someone with a defaulted second mortgage come up with a lump sum of $6,200? A common source of capital that many homeowners are not aware of is their 401(k) or other retirement accounts. In many instances, these funds can be accessed without penalty or tax consequences to address delinquent mortgage debt on a primary residence. Loans from friends and family or the sale of a second or third car are other examples of raising capital. Getting an upfront chunk of money not only greatly enhances returns, but also sends a strong signal of commitment by the homeowner to the newly modified loan conditions.

In this example, the note company recouped nearly all of its initial investment after year one, and assuming payments remain steady, it can hold on to this asset long term and realize annual returns of 41 percent! Just like an experienced rehabber can physically renovate a property, its finances be rehabbed as well.

Keep in mind, however, that these specialty funds have to buy these distressed notes in large unfiltered pools from banks, and many will result in much more modest returns or none at all. This again underscores the importance of diversification.

Property Information

Fair market value: $120,000

First mortgage: $114,000 (current)

Note Purchase Information

Note purchase price: $10,850 (paid 20 percent of UPB)

Collection and filing fees: $1,091

Total invested in the deal: $11,941

Arrears/back payments collected upfront: $6,291

Workout: Unpaid principal balance: $53,799.62
Thirty-year loan at 3 percent
Monthly payment: $408.11

Return on Investment
Amount earned in first year: $11,188.32
Recoup of original investment in first year: 94 percent
(11,188.32/11,941)
Annual internal rate of return: 41 percent ([408.11 ×
12] / 11,941)

Distressed notes represent a less well-known but potentially very profitable way to participate in real estate for the savvy investor. Though these notes have always been more of a niche market, the mortgage crisis has primed the pump with a robust amount of inventory that should provide ample opportunity for years. My hope is that you are intrigued enough to further your education and gain the confidence to make your first note investment.

As much as I like notes, it's time to move on to another real estate investment I consider even better: rental property. Let's learn why owning income property is my preferred asset class and the cornerstone of my long-term wealth-building strategy.

Chapter 7

Hassle-Free Rentals

All the Benefits of Rental Property Income, with Less Hassle

Consider the following quotations from some of the earliest and biggest business titans in the history of this country.

> *"The major fortunes in America have been made in land."*
> —John D. Rockefeller

> *"Ninety percent of all millionaires become so through owning real estate. More money has been made in real estate than in all industrial investments combined. The wise young man or wage earner of today invests his money in real estate."*
> —Andrew Carnegie

"Buy on the fringe and wait. Buy land near a growing city! Buy real estate when other people want to sell. Hold what you buy!"
—John Jacob Astor, America's first millionaire

When most people think of Rockefeller and Carnegie, oil and steel probably come immediately to mind, but they were heavily involved in real estate as well. John Jacob Astor, of Waldorf Astoria fame, is credited with being the first millionaire in America. He made his initial fortune in fur trapping among other ventures but soon after became one of the wealthiest landholders in New York.

You don't have to be a financial guru to know intuitively that land and real estate is a good investment in general. It's tangible, unlike a traditional paper asset such as a stock or bond. It's nonrenewable and limited, as expressed so eloquently by Mark Twain: "Buy land, they aren't making any more of it!" Last but not least, it has intrinsic value. As long as there are humans on this earth, we will always have the need for shelter.

Real estate, and more specifically property ownership, is the one asset class I know of that can uniquely combine four key wealth-accelerating attributes. I use the acronym T.A.L.C to remember them:

Tax advantages: Essentially all of the necessary expenses associated with owning and maintaining the real estate asset can be written off. Additionally, there are significant depreciation benefits where annually you get to write off part of the value of the asset.

Appreciation: The potential for the asset to increase in value and therefore be sold at a higher price than when it was initially purchased. For my style of investing, I consider this to be a welcome bonus, but not a core strategy.

Leverage: The ability to control an asset with all the benefits of ownership while putting up only a fraction of the total purchase price. In normal times, a 20 percent down payment with the remainder being financed by a bank is a typical scenario.

Cash flow: Income generated from the use of the property, usually expressed as monthly rent. This is the main goal of my investment strategy and forms the primary lens through which I evaluate potential target acquisitions.

Once I decided to get into property ownership, the next natural question became what type of property. The potential choices are quite varied, ranging from farmland to mobile homes, commercial buildings, apartments, and more.

Like many first-time investors, I chose to focus on single-family homes, as it seemed to be the easiest asset type to understand. As Warren Buffet, widely considered to be the greatest investor of all time, says, invest only in things you truly understand.

I committed to learning as much about single-family homes as I could through many books, podcasts, webinars, and meetings. What I discovered was a whole host of societal factors that were very favorable to the long-term prospects of rental property as an investment.

> *Psychographic:* This is a fancy term reflecting the shift in mental attitude around homeownership. Its place as a cornerstone of the American financial dream is slowly diminishing for a variety of factors.

Many people are still dealing with repercussions of the greatest mortgage crisis this country has ever seen in the form of foreclosures and bankruptcies and are reluctant to take on another mortgage. On the other side, banks and financial situations have returned to much stricter lending standards as well.

Given the much more fragmented and temporary nature of work, particularly among the millennial demographic, geographic mobility has emerged as a very important lifestyle feature. This is much more conducive to renting.

Student debt: At a staggering 1.3 <u>trillion</u> dollars, student loan debt is now larger than credit card debt and has major implications that resonate throughout society. Young adults saddled with large debt burdens often delay marriage and family formation, which is a major trigger for home purchases. When coupled with a shaky job market and stagnant wages, many cannot qualify for traditional mortgages and will be long-term renters.

Baby boomers: They have actually accounted for more than half of all the rental demand in the past ten years. Many have opted to downsize into smaller homes, apartments, and condominiums, relieving themselves of the burdens of ownership. Additionally, they value not having their money tied to a mortgage.

The more I learned, two very definitive conclusions emerged:

1. Single-family homes could certainly be the cornerstone of my long-term wealth-building strategy.

2. I didn't have the time or expertise needed to be an active investor dealing with ongoing management of a property portfolio.

Fortunately, through my research I also discovered the turnkey rental model.

How It Works

While there is no universally agreed-upon definition of what a turnkey company is, in general it handles all or nearly all of the aspects involved in the acquisition and ongoing ownership of rental property. This includes identifying, buying, renovating, and managing the property long term. When considering the vastness of the overall real estate investing market, it is very much a cottage industry that has gained momentum over the past several years.

Turnkey companies tend to market themselves to higher-net-worth individuals who don't mind paying a premium for a hands-off passive investing experience.

Some turnkey providers specialize in smaller multifamily properties, but single-family homes are the most popular investment vehicle for this model. Most commonly, a full-service turnkey provider starts off by acquiring below-market—usually distressed—properties. Then the provider puts in the work to rehabilitate those properties and ideally place a well-screened, low-risk tenant. Once a signed lease and a security deposit have been secured, that's typically when the investor is engaged.

The investor assumes control of the property, either

through a cash purchase or through financing sometimes arranged by the turnkey company. Some providers even have relationships with banks and preferred lenders to help facilitate the transaction.

Because a tenant is already in place and cash is coming in, there's no lag for the investor/owner to start seeing returns.

How to Get Started

Picking a Property

The best single piece of advice I can offer you is to make sure you use the 1 percent rule. That means that your monthly rental amount should be equal to at least 1 percent of your total purchase price for that property. This sets you up for a positive cash flow after accounting for debt service and routine expenses.

According to the US Census Bureau's data from 2013, most renters pay between $800 and $1,100 per month, with the national median at $905. If we apply our 1 percent rule here, that narrows our target price range for rental properties to between $80,000 and $110,000. Barring vacancies or the need for expensive repairs, earning 1 percent monthly means you should be making a gross annual return of 12 percent of your initial investment.

Markets in the Midwest (e.g., Ohio, Indiana, Kansas City, and Memphis) are popular in my experience, because you can still buy properties within the ideal price range. This means that even if you take out a loan to acquire the property, your debt service is such that generally the property still generates positive cash flow for you. Obviously, depending on where you live, a high level of comfort with owning property outside of your immediate locale may be required. This underscores the paramount importance of having good property management in place.

Another thing to consider is the neighborhood. In the real estate investment community, specific neighborhoods are ranked A, B, C, or D. Generally, you want to aim for a B neighborhood—a middle-class community with a good mix of owners and renters. The bulk of properties conforming to the 1 percent rule will be found there. A neighborhoods are going to be too expensive, and C and D neighborhoods aren't attractive to the kind of stable, low-risk renters you're targeting.

While you want to buy properties at a good price, as a general rule you don't want to buy very inexpensive homes in the $30,000 to $40,000 range and lower. On paper, a $35,000 property that rents for $750 produces returns of greater than 2 percent per month, giving the impression that they are cash flow machines. But there are some serious factors to consider. Unfortunately, these properties are often plagued by neighborhood, tenant, and property issues that can substantially decrease your returns.

I have targeted three-bedroom, two-bathroom homes in

B neighborhoods in Jacksonville, Florida, catering to dual-income middle-class families. This tenant profile tends to rent for longer durations, hence minimizing what is often the largest expense associated with investment property: turnover and vacancy.

Try to avoid properties that are located near commercial districts or multifamily dwellings such as apartment complexes. Neighborhoods with schools, parks, and churches are preferred, and ideally at least 50 percent of the properties are occupied by homeowners, to enhance community stability.

My properties thus far have had an average cost of $75,000 each, and they rent for $1,000, translating to a 1.33 percent return per month and an annual *cash-on-cash* return of 16 percent ($12,000/$75,000). This annual return is enhanced once you factor in tax write-offs such as depreciation, insurance, property taxes, and management costs.

Figure 1 shows an example of a monthly cash-flow projection for a turnkey property, also known as a proforma. These are prominently featured on many sites and function as a useful aid in investment decisions on an individual property. Some components, such as taxes and management fees, can vary considerably by location and provider. Others, such as vacancy and repairs, are true projections wherein you might not incur any actual expenses during a particular year but should still budget for them.

I like to allocate at least 5 percent of the rent to each of these categories as a reserve, while others opt for 10 percent. The other big variable expense is debt service, if you take out a loan to buy the property. Assuming you obtain reasonable financing terms, your monthly cash-flow number is often cut in half compared with a cash purchase. The overall investment return percentage increases, however, due to the power of leverage.

Figure 1: Sample proforma on a cash purchase of a turnkey property. If financed, the projected cash flow would be decreased by approximately half.

Turnkey Property Sale Price	$ 75,000
Projected Rent	$ 1,000
Projected Taxes	$ 160
Projected Insurance	$ 50
PM Fee 8%	$ 80
Projected Maintenance 5%	$ 50
Projected Vacancy Rate 5%	$ 50
Projected Cash Flow	$ 610

Proformas, even when constructed by knowledgeable and conscientious real estate professionals, are ultimately projections. So how did my first rental property actually perform during my first year of ownership?

Here are the actual numbers on my first turnkey property, purchased without any debt in June 2014. With a price of $75,000 and monthly rent of exactly $1,000, this translates into a 1.33 percent return per month, which easily meets the 1 percent rule. After all expenses have been subtracted from the rent, this leaves an annual net income of $9,047. Dividing this number by the purchase price gives us a 12.1 percent cash-on-cash return. *Cash-on-cash return* refers to how much cash you receive for the amount you have to spend. It doesn't take into account potential tax and depreciation savings, which can increase your actual returns significantly, but nonetheless it is a quick and easy metric you can use as a starting point. I aim for a level of at least 10 percent.

Figure 2: The actual first-year numbers on my first turnkey rental property

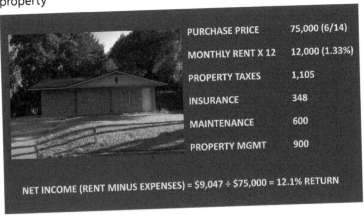

PURCHASE PRICE	75,000 (6/14)
MONTHLY RENT X 12	12,000 (1.33%)
PROPERTY TAXES	1,105
INSURANCE	348
MAINTENANCE	600
PROPERTY MGMT	900

NET INCOME (RENT MINUS EXPENSES) = $9,047 ÷ $75,000 = 12.1% RETURN

Based on a review of the turnkey inventory offered by a number of providers, the average price of a home is between $60,000 and $120,000. Access to that much capital—through either your own cash reserves or financing—is what you need initially to get started.

Personally, I tapped into my network of family and friends by taking on private loans from them in order to finance my properties. Provided the properties are purchased at an attractive price and perform as expected, I can afford to pay the people in my network an attractive return on their money (8.0 percent) while still receiving positive monthly cash flow from rents.

Online Resources

Once you've determined that turnkey real estate investment is something you're definitely interested in, there are plenty of online resources you can use to identify both the right market and the right turnkey team for you. Some of these include the following:

- **Turnkey-reviews.com**

  I particularly like this site, because it's chock full of detailed reviews from people who have done business with specific turnkey providers. Being able to hear from people who have experience working with a provider before you put feelers out to that company makes for an invaluable resource. I was fortunate enough to be a guest on the site's podcast, and I hope my insights were helpful to other investors.

- **BiggerPockets.com**

  This site is full of information on all aspects of real estate, including turnkey rentals. They have a very active user forum with a wealth of useful insights from both owner/investors and providers. Additionally, the site owners host regular webinars that often cover topics relevant to rental property ownership.

- **RealWeatlhNetwork.com**

  Kathy Fettke and her team maintain an affiliate relationship with select turnkey providers throughout the country. They deserve to be highlighted for publishing their set of rehab standards that must be met before recommending a property to their investor network. I highly recommend visiting their site to review this list as part of your general education about turnkey investing.

  Roof: Replaced if less than ten years of life left, approved by an independent home inspection

  Furnace, boiler, A/C: Replaced if less than five years of life left, certified by an HVAC contractor

Plumbing: Updated, and approved per independent home inspection

Hot water heater: Replaced if less than five years of life left or if the home was vacant for six months, certified by a licensed plumber

Foundation: Approved per independent home inspection

Electric: Updated and approved per independent home inspection

Driveways: Safety, approved per independent home inspection and city requirements

Flooring: Updated with durable products (commercial vinyl tile, ceramic tile, laminate, hardwood—carpet not recommended)

Interior paint: Freshly painted (semi-gloss recommended)

Exterior paint: Repaint, or touch up if exterior has been painted in last five years

Fixtures: Updated lighting, switches, blinds, fixtures, cabinet hardware, doorknobs—all to level of neighborhood

Appliances: Replace/update dishwasher, garbage disposal, stove, refrigerator, washer, dryer to neighborhood level and tenant expectation

These sites all provide easily accessible and highly relevant information and make for a great starting point.

Due Diligence and Pitfalls to Watch Out For

As with any investment, there are some potential downsides.

Liquidity

Unlike a stock, which can be sold instantly with the push of a keystroke, a rental home could take weeks to months to sell depending on local market conditions. I am very much a buy-and-hold investor for the long term, and you should certainly be comfortable with a time horizon potentially measured in years before committing to a rental home.

Problem Tenant

The potential ways a problem tenant can make your ownership experience a real headache vary from non-payment of rent to outright vandalism. The ease with which you can legally remove such a tenant range widely from state to state. In so-called "landlord friendly" states, this can be accomplished in a matter of a few weeks. Alternatively, in "tenant friendly" states, savvy tenants can exploit legal provisions to stretch this process out for months and devastate your investment returns.

Liability

If a tenant has a slip and fall, or a tree falls on the house, you as the owner are ultimately responsible. Proper physical maintenance of the property and a good insurance policy are a must.

Pick a Market

When you begin your due diligence process before you buy, the first thing you want to decide is what markets you're interested in.

As mentioned, the Midwest is popular because house prices there fit well with this business model. You can certainly find good deals in select neighborhoods of bigger cities nationwide as well. However, in huge cities, the majority of real estate isn't going to fit the turnkey model because it's simply too expensive.

For me, proximity was and still is a concern. I'm only about an hour away from Jacksonville. Even though this is a relatively hands-off investment, it gives me peace of mind to know that if something big *were* to go wrong, I could hop in the car and get there fairly quickly. That might matter less to other people, but for me, it's a comfort thing.

Turnkey Reviews makes it particularly easy to get useful demographic data. Once you're logged in, you can click on specific target markets—Atlanta, for instance—to drill down and get quick access to basic information about them, such as median income, the percentage of homes that are rented vs. bought, typical rents for different kinds of units, and crime statistics. Zillow, Trulia, and the local MLS can give you a reasonable price estimate of comparable homes near the target property being considered.

Find the Best Turnkey Provider for Your Market

And finally, you want to make sure you pick a reputable, top-notch turnkey company to work with.

One thing to keep in mind is that turnkey companies often acquire distressed properties that need at least some work, because there's more profit in it for them if they can get that property cheaper. Now, they're not going in there putting in marble countertops and hardwood floors—they're just performing rental-grade rehab. That said, a good turnkey provider will take care to minimize the risk of having a big maintenance issue come up.

That means that if the home needs big-ticket items such as new plumbing or a new roof, these should be taken care of *before* the investor is brought onboard.

Good turnkey companies know that the key to their success is creating a good long-term relationship between them and you, the investor. They know that if the first house you buy from them begins with a relatively smooth transaction and continues with minimum hassle on your part, you might be inclined to buy multiple properties with them down the road.

In contrast, bad turnkey providers do shoddy, cheap rehabs that cause problems and adversely affect the returns of their investors. The people who have been burned by these companies aren't shy about saying so on the platforms I mentioned earlier. So make sure to do your homework on a provider on these sites before you start doing business with it.

It's also best to go with a provider that intends to stick around as your property manager after you buy the property. Again, you want someone committed to a long-term relationship with you and your money, as opposed to someone just out to make a quick buck, who has no incentive to care what happens to that property or its new owner once the deed changes hands.

When it comes time to vet a turnkey company, it's always a good idea to read online reviews and talk to other investors who have experience working with that company. Key things to get a gauge on are the company's timeliness both in response to tenant complaints and in communication with the owner.

You may also choose to do a site visit, which should include a tour of the company's operating headquarters. Because most of these companies provide ongoing property management services, you want to see evidence of the robust and systematized in-place practices necessary to manage a large number of units. Increasingly, some of the larger providers are offering robust online portals where owners can log on and see in near real time items such as the rent deposits and repair invoices.

It's also a good idea to do a field tour, where you can inspect both established and newly acquired properties to get a sense of the quality of the renovations the company is doing.

Once a certain level of comfort is achieved with a provider, usually after a few purchases, this process can be radically streamlined. In fact, I have talked to a number of investors who now buy their properties from trusted turn-key companies after just a brief perusal of Internet pictures and the proforma—even if the home is halfway across the country!

Hire a Third-Party Appraiser and Inspector

Another thing I recommend is due diligence on specific properties before you buy them. Hire your own third-party appraiser and inspector for each rental property *before* you make a purchase. It's important that the turnkey company make a profit, but you certainly don't want to pay more than market value for the home, and that's where the appraiser comes in. In fact, if you use conventional financing, the bank will require this in any event. Some turnkey companies make an effort to sell the property below market price to provide the investor with instant equity, which is a great place to start.

The home inspection is important particularly to verify the renovations and potentially discover (hopefully) smaller repair issues to be addressed before the investor takes possession of the home.

While the turnkey company may offer to refer you to its preferred inspectors and appraisers, I think it is always a good idea to get your own. Otherwise, there is great potential for conflicts of interest and collusion at the investor's expense.

When it comes to your money and your future security, it's much better to be safe than sorry.

So How Hassle Free Is It Really?

Well, consider the following facts:

1. I very rarely visit my properties physically even though they are only about an hour away. For some, the only time I have ever seen them was a one-time visual inspection immediately prior to purchasing them.

2. I have no contact or interaction with my tenants. They don't know that I am the owner, and they call the property manager with any problems. If it weren't for seeing their rental applications and pay-stubs, I wouldn't even know their names.

3. I am called only for big issues, such as repairs above a certain price point, rent nonpayment/potential eviction, and modifying lease terms. If we stick to our fundamentals of having a well-renovated property with a properly screened tenant, these issues will come up very sporadically.

Conclusion

Purchased at the right price from the right provider, turnkey properties are a great way to get exposure to the tremendous wealth-building opportunities of real estate ownership without the hassles of day-to-day management.

I hope to have piqued your interest enough in this asset class so that you will continue your exploration and learning. A few years ago, I knew absolutely nothing about real estate investing. Now, I am planning to make it the foundation of my retirement plan and financial legacy to my children. That's how much I believe in it, and I hope one day you will as well.

Chapter 8

Student Loan Investing

Multiple Generations Burdened with Debt

The cost of college tuition has skyrocketed over the last twenty years, which has led to a rise in the need for student loans. As a result, student loan debt—a market currently valued at $1.3 trillion—is now the second highest form of debt in the United States, behind only mortgage debt. And that market valuation is still on the rise.

Tuition cost and consequently student debt has exploded over past fifteen years in particular

College Cost Increases Since 1980

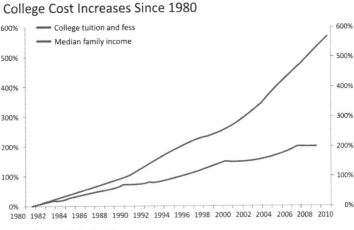

Source: Bureau of Labor Statistics

Now, you might think of the average person struggling to pay down student loan debt as someone in his or her twenties, thirties, or forties. But the reality is that, today, even senior citizens are laboring under this burden—and on a fixed income, that's not pretty. Between 2005 and 2013, student loan debt among seniors sixty-five and older rose by more than 600 percent—from $2.8 billion to $18 billion, according to a new report from the Government Accountability Office. One key reason this debt lingers is that, generally speaking, it is very difficult to discharge student loans, even in bankruptcy. The impact of student loans on the lives of those saddled with them is huge. People deep in such debt typically delay major life milestones, such as purchasing a home or starting a family, far later than their peers do.

Plus, high interest rates on these kinds of loans are commonplace, meaning that borrowers are paying more for their loans, in addition to paying longer and later into life. This is an increasingly widespread problem, and people paying high-interest student loans need workable alternatives to help them get out of debt faster and at lower interest rates. Seeing an opportunity, online lending platforms such as SoFi and CommonBond have entered the student loan market to help creditworthy borrowers refinance their student loans at a lower rate. In the process, their investors are making a profit, while still providing borrowers with the opportunity to save a lot of money.

Because these kinds of platforms focus on refinancing loans for borrowers with low-risk credit histories and high employability, the investor returns are more modest. If you're looking for a high return and are comfortable with higher risk, this might not be the best avenue for you. But if you're looking to diversify into something very safe, this kind of investment could work well as part of your portfolio. In this chapter, we'll cover the ins and outs of entering the student loan refinancing market, including how it compares with other types of investments, pitfalls to watch out for, and best practices.

How It Works

One of the problems with the current student loan underwriting system is that, well, there isn't really any underwriting. People who have better credit histories and employment chances don't get better rates than anybody else. Intuitively, we know that a graduate from Stanford Business School is a better credit risk than a student at an online or for-profit school, where the dropout and loan default rates are much higher. So why should they both get the same interest rates? That's exactly what Stanford Business School graduates Mike Cagney and Dan Macklin thought, and it prompted them to start SoFi, a company poised to disrupt the student debt industry.

Cagney and Macklin went to the people most intimately familiar with how creditworthy a Stanford MBA is—the alumni. And they learned that not a single graduate from their program had ever defaulted on his or her student loans. Now, these are finance guys, and this got them thinking, "Well, hey. Why can't we put together a fund that would refinance this group's student loans?" That's how the company started, and it has only grown from there. The founders of SoFi put together a pilot program wherein forty alums raised $2 million to refinance a hundred recent graduates in 2011. The program was a success and has prompted significant outside investment from venture capitalists, to the tune of hundreds of millions of dollars. As of late 2016, the company has funded more than $9 billion in loans.

How SoFi Works

A typical borrower comes to the platform with a legacy interest rate from the government or a private lender in the 6.5 percent to 7.9 percent range. SoFi is able to routinely refinance these legacy rates to new rates in the 4 percent to 5 percent range. While that may not sound like much, when you consider the average debt load is $80,000, this translates into a savings of approximately $14,000 over the maximum twenty-year life of one of these loans.

As of this writing, the founders claim there has never even been a delinquency, let alone a default. Notably, a big reason for delinquencies and defaults in general is job loss. And that's where the folks behind SoFi have done something very smart. If a SoFi borrower has employment issues, he or she has the unique opportunity to reach out to the alumni network for references and job referrals. This has been an, if somewhat unanticipated, nonetheless large component of the success for this business model. The founders note that there seems to be an increased incentive not to default if the borrower feels connected to the lender around a common community—in many cases with SoFi loans, the alumni network for a particular school.

Besides help with jobs, borrowers can also get formal mentorship and support if, for instance, they are in the process of launching a startup company. Another huge factor in SoFi's success is the favorable financial profile of these borrowers. For starters, a borrower has to have a job or a confirmed job offer in hand to be eligible for loan refinancing. Currently, SoFi limits its product to graduates of approximately two hundred top schools who majored in fields of study associated with high rates of employment and income. Specifically, they favor business, law, engineering, and medicine. The average income of a borrower is $120,000, compared to the median US household income of approximately $56,000.

This exceptionally high level of safety is easily the single largest benefit of this type of investment. It's also a nice way to diversify if you're attracted to the idea of doing some social good with your money while earning a modest return—because you're also helping to provide a valuable, money-saving service to people with high-interest student loan debt. More recently, SoFi has begun leveraging the favorable borrower experience into a more full-service financial relationship. It now provides mortgages in select states, as well as personal loans and wealth management services in addition to its flagship student loan offerings. The other market leader in this space, CommonBond, operates in a fundamentally similar way.

Next, let's look at what you'll need to get started in

this kind of investing, plus online platforms and other resources you can use to become better educated about these products.

How to Get Started

Things are rapidly changing in the world of online alternative lending, and for full disclosure, the particular opportunity I invested in is no longer available for individuals but rather for institutions. Nonetheless, I think it is instructive to review the specifics of the offering, as it will likely serve as a template for other opportunities that arise in this space.

While SoFi had only been around since 2011, it had an excellent track record among its borrowers and offered a novel investment vehicle granting access to prime student debt. At the time I joined the platform in 2015, it offered a specialty fund open to accredited investors with a $10,000 minimum. The money was then disbursed among a diverse group of qualified students to refinance their debt. The fund offered a return of 4 percent multiplied by the percentage of loans that are performing. As of this writing, that percentage is 99.2 percent!

If you contrast that with the number of borrowers who default on student loans from the government (4 percent to 5 percent) or from private lenders (closer to 13 percent), it clearly validates the underwriting process. The returns are paid quarterly, and the term of the investment is five years.

You could have, if desired, invested in a pool of borrowers from a specific school or participated in the "all school pool." Given the overall quality of the applicants, I chose the latter option.

SoFi's fund incorporated the marketplace mechanism, small capital requirements, and due diligence common to the other online alternative lenders detailed previously.

Risks

When weighing whether this kind of investment is right for you, here are a few important things to consider:

1. The possibility of an economic downturn. This would lead to an increase in defaults in general. I would argue that platforms such as SoFi and CommonBond would weather this better than most, given the upward mobility of their clientele.

2. Low liquidity. There is no robust secondary market for investments of this type yet, so in my case I have to plan to hold it for the entire five-year duration.

3. Competition. If private lenders (or the government in particular) added a similar level of underwriting sophistication to their student loan products, they could easily overwhelm these specialty platforms. Personally, I view this as the biggest risk.

Leveraging Returns and Social Good

One more thing important to mention about this type of investment is that SoFi represents a social impact investment for me—meaning I am willing to take a lower rate of return in exchange for some social good. The SoFi fund's maximum return is in the 4 percent range, which is substantially less than any other opportunity discussed in this book. That said, it is still a much better return than you'll see with a savings account. Given this and the overall low risk, considering the financial profile of the borrower, I think refinancing student loans is worth looking into. The people I'm helping have worked hard to better themselves through education, and their hard work and diligence have further paid off in attaining a good credit history. Helping them while still making a return is what I call a true win-win.

From talking to management at these platforms, I am confident opportunities like the SoFi fund will eventually be available again to the individual investor. Therefore, I would encourage you to periodically check their sites for updates. Alternatively, you may still have some student loan debt that could benefit from a refinance. While technically not an investment in the traditional sense, it could nonetheless potentially yield a significant return.

Chapter 9

Your Future, Your Way

An Alternative Financial Future—Starting Today

As you have seen, there are numerous places to put your money that are free of the toxic combination of volatility and low yield that has plagued many of our portfolios for too long. Inflation-beating returns, security, and an unprecedented level of access to heretofore unavailable asset classes is very possible.

While rental property is the cornerstone of my wealth-building strategy, personally I am most excited about what the emerging online lending platforms represent. I believe we are on the verge of a massive sea change in the way investment opportunities and financial services are available and delivered. And if you are willing to embrace that, you can reap the benefits of this transformational change in how investments work. As several of the opportunities discussed in this book illustrate, there is a new freedom and connectivity age emerging, where your money will be able to flow to whoever and whatever needs it without the traditional middlemen.

The flexibility you can achieve in your investments today is like nothing you've seen before. As I've shown you, you can direct where you want your money to go—from the neighborhood coffee shop to a multimillion-dollar apartment building across the country. And you can make those kinds of decisions from anywhere, using your computer or your phone. It will take some work on your part to educate yourself further on each type of opportunity of interest to you. But the resources I've pointed you to have everything you need to make that transition and to start making investments that are smarter, faster, safer, and more flexible. Some of the opportunities discussed in this book are currently available only to accredited investors, but legislation is in the works to allow everyone to participate, so your task is to get educated and participate.

My hope is that this book will serve as an important first step. Ultimately, I want you to be part of my online community at www.AlternativeFinancialMedicine.com. There, I will continue to provide value by bringing on the many industry experts who are part of my network to give you professional insight into these opportunities. You'll find regular updates, blog posts, and videos, as well as information about new opportunities and platforms. Of course, I will continue to document my ongoing participation and results, so you can benefit from my experiences—both the good and the bad.

I know that some of you will eventually take the plunge and open a peer lending account, participate in a house flip, or buy a property in part based on what you have learned here, and we certainly want to hear about it when you do. So definitely visit the site, YouTube channel, or Facebook group and post your story or any questions you have.

As recently as a few years ago, I hadn't even heard of many of the opportunities in this manuscript; indeed, some of them didn't exist. They now make up a significant portion of my assets. My whole investment philosophy and outlook has changed after an extensive amount of hard work, networking, and learning, and the benefits for me and for my family have been tremendous. The level of diversification and returns achieved thus far gives me peace of mind as well as optimism for the future. Hopefully, this text starts you down that path as well.

Let's see what your money can do for you—not just when you're ready to retire, but here. Now. Today. Happy learning. Happy investing. And God bless you.

ABOUT THE AUTHOR

KENYON MEADOWS, MD is a practicing Radiation Oncologist and alternative investment enthusiast.

Sparked by discussions with older colleagues who had their retirement timelines extended by the 2008 downturn, Meadows Enterprises was launched in 2013 with the goal of investing in high yield alternative assets uncorrelated to the stock market. After beginning with traditional private mortgage lending, the company quickly embraced the online financial technology platforms emerging in peer lending, real estate crowdfunding, and more. Alternative Financial Medicine was born out a desire to inform fellow investors about the wide range of options available to help them achieve true diversification and inflation beating yields. His insights have been featured on MSN Money, and Alternative Investment Coach.

Dr. Meadows is a native of Youngstown, Ohio and is

a graduate of Case Western Reserve University, where he received a BA and MD.

Kenyon is married to Wilnita Meadows and has 2 children, Camille and Gabrielle. He lives in St. Simons Island, GA.

When not busy treating cancer patients and spending time with family, he can be found soaking up all the podcasts, books, and conferences on alternative investing he can.

86899930R00066

Made in the USA
Middletown, DE
31 August 2018